Faith in Motion

Connecting Spirit and Body

Faith in Motion

Connecting Spirit and Body

A 30-Day Practice of Scripture, Reflection, and Yoga

Taprea Cardaa

To you, precious reader –

This journey is as much yours as it is mine.
May each page bring you closer to the peace, strength, and grace that lies within you. As you connect spirit and body through these daily practices, may you find the love, light, and purpose that God has uniquely placed within your heart.

Thank you for allowing me to walk alongside you on this path of Faith in Motion.

With deep gratitude,
Taprea Cardaa

CONTENTS

Introduction

Welcome to "Faith in Motion: Connecting Spirit and Body." I'm excited to share this journey with you, blending the power of scripture with the practice of yoga. Our daily lives can often feel overwhelming, and it's easy to lose sight of our spiritual connection. This devotional is designed to help you find a moment of peace, reflection, and physical alignment each day.

In these pages, you'll discover daily themes that draw from the wisdom of the Bible, paired with yoga poses that enhance your physical and spiritual well-being. Each day will guide you through a scripture, a thoughtful reflection, a yoga pose, and practical applications to integrate the day's message into your life. Whether you're new to yoga or an experienced practitioner, this devotional is for anyone seeking to deepen their faith and nurture their body. As you move through each day, take the time to reflect, breathe, and allow God's word to speak to your heart.

I encourage you to approach this journey with an open mind and a willing spirit. Together, we'll explore how to live out our faith in both stillness and motion. Let's embark on this path to connect more deeply with God and ourselves.

In many spiritual traditions, including Christianity, the garden is a powerful symbol of growth, renewal, and communion with God. The Bible begins in a garden, the Garden of Eden, where God and humanity walked together in harmony. Gardens represent a place of cultivation, where seeds are planted and nurtured, eventually bearing fruit. This mirrors our spiritual journey—nurturing our faith, growing in our relationship with God, and producing the fruits of the Spirit in our lives (Galatians 5:22-23).

Similarly, in yoga, nature, and especially plants, are seen as symbols of life, growth, and balance. Just as a plant needs the right conditions to thrive—light, water, and care—so do we need spiritual practices, such as prayer, meditation, and movement, to nourish our body, mind, and spirit.

Throughout this devotional, the plants and garden imagery serve as a reminder of our ongoing journey of growth in faith and the continual process of aligning ourselves with God's purpose. As you move through each day, allow these symbols to inspire you to cultivate your inner garden, nurturing the seeds of faith, peace, and connection with every breath, prayer, and yoga pose.

Purpose and Vision

The purpose of this devotional is to weave together the power of God's word with the physical practice of yoga, cultivating a holistic approach to daily devotion. Each day, you will be invited to meditate on a scripture that speaks to various aspects of faith, love, strength, and resilience. Paired with these scriptures are yoga poses that embody the essence of the day's message, helping you to integrate these spiritual truths into your body and mind.

Yoga, with its emphasis on mindful movement and breath, provides a perfect complement to spiritual reflection. As you stretch and strengthen your body, you'll also be stretching and strengthening your faith, creating a deeper connection between your spirit and your physical being. This devotional aims to nurture both your soul and your body, helping you to live out your faith in a more embodied and intentional way.

How to Use This Devotional

To get the most out of this devotional, I encourage you to set aside a dedicated time each day for your practice.

1. Find a Quiet Space: Choose a peaceful spot where you can focus without distractions. This could be a corner of your home, a spot in the park, or anywhere you feel comfortable and serene.

2. Begin with Prayer: Start your practice with a moment of prayer, inviting God's presence into your time of devotion. Ask for guidance, peace, and an open heart to receive His word.

3. Read the Scripture: Each day begins with a scripture. Take your time reading it, letting the words sink into your heart. Reflect on what it means to you personally.

4. Reflect: Read the reflection provided for the day. Consider how the scripture applies to your life and what God might be saying to you through it. You might want to journal your thoughts or simply meditate on the message.

5. Practice the Yoga Pose: Move into the yoga pose that corresponds with the day's theme. Follow the instructions carefully, focusing on your breath and the sensations in your body. Allow the pose to help you embody the day's message.

6. Application: Finally, consider the practical application of the day's message. How can you live out this truth in your daily life? This might involve a specific action, a change in mindset, or a new habit to cultivate.

7. Meditate and Pray: End your session with a few moments of meditation and prayer. Thank God for the insights and strength you've gained, and ask for His continued guidance as you carry the day's message into your life.

By dedicating this time each day, you'll find yourself growing stronger both spiritually and physically. Let this devotional be a tool for deepening your relationship with God and nurturing your body as a temple of the Holy Spirit.
Blessings, Taprea

Day 1: Trust in the Lord
Scripture: Proverbs 3:5-6

"Trust in the Lord with all your heart and lean not on your own understanding; in all your ways submit to him, and he will make your paths straight."

Reflection:

Trusting God's plan over our understanding can be challenging. Yet, when we surrender our worries and doubts to Him, we find peace and direction. Reflect on areas in your life where you need to let go and trust God more fully.

Yoga Pose: Mountain Pose (Tadasana)

Pose Description:
- Stand tall with your feet together, shoulders relaxed, weight evenly distributed through your soles, arms at your sides.
- Take a deep breath and raise your hands overhead, palms facing each other.
- Reach for the sky with your fingertips while grounding down through your feet.

Application:
- Start your day by acknowledging trust in God.
- List three areas where you can surrender control to Him.
- Practice Mountain Pose, focusing on grounding yourself in faith.

Prayer:

"Lord, help me to trust in You with all my heart. When I am tempted to lean on my own understanding, guide me back to Your truth. I surrender my worries and doubts to You, trusting that You will make my paths straight. Amen."

Day 2: God's Strength
Scripture: Philippians 4:13
"I can do all things through him who gives me strength."

Reflection:
Drawing strength from Christ means relying on Him in all circumstances, not just in moments of weakness. Consider where you need God's strength today and how you can lean on Him fully.

Yoga Pose: Warrior II (Virabhadrasana II)
Pose Description:
• Stand with your feet wide apart. Turn your right foot out 90 degrees and your left foot slightly in.
• Bend your right knee over your right ankle, keeping your left leg straight.
• Raise your arms parallel to the floor, reaching out through your fingertips.
• Focus your gaze over your right hand, embodying the strength and determination that comes from Christ.

Application:
• Identify areas in your life where you need God's strength.
• Reflect on past moments when His strength has carried you through.
• Practice Warrior II, channeling that strength as you hold the pose.

Meditation:
Take a few deep breaths, and with each inhale, imagine God's strength filling you. With each exhale, release any feelings of weakness or fear. Repeat the affirmation: "I can do all things through Christ who strengthens me."

Day 3: Faith and Action
Scripture: James 2:17
"In the same way, faith by itself, if it is not accompanied by action, is dead."

Reflection:

Faith is not passive; it's active and alive. It requires us to step out and take action, even when we're unsure of the outcome. Reflect on the ways you can put your faith into action today.

Yoga Pose: Downward-Facing Dog (Adho Mukha Svanasana)
Pose Description:

• Start on your hands and knees. Spread your fingers wide, pressing firmly into your hands.
• Tuck your toes and lift your hips up and back, forming an inverted V-shape with your body.
• Keep your knees slightly bent if needed, and focus on pressing your chest towards your thighs.
• Downward-Facing Dog represents both strength and surrender, embodying the balance of faith and action.

Application:

• Write down one action you can take today to live out your faith.
• Reflect on how God has called you to act in faith in the past.
• Practice Downward-Facing Dog, focusing on the balance between effort and release.

Prayer:
"Father, give me the courage to act on my faith today. Show me where I need to step out and trust You, and help me to take those steps with boldness and conviction. Let my actions reflect my faith in You. Amen."

Day 4: God's Love
Scripture: 1 John 4:16

"And so we know and rely on the love God has for us. God is love. Whoever lives in love lives in God, and God in them."

Reflection:

Living in God's love means embodying that love in our interactions with others. Reflect on how you can be a vessel of God's love today, showing kindness, patience, and compassion.

Yoga Pose: Child's Pose (Balasana)

Pose Description:
- Kneel on the floor, touching your big toes together and sitting back on your heels.
- Lower your torso between your knees, extending your arms forward or resting them alongside your body.
- Focus on your breath, allowing yourself to rest in God's love, feeling His embrace as you surrender into the pose.

Application:
- Reflect on how you can show God's love to others today.
- Consider ways you can be more loving, patient, and compassionate.
- Practice Child's Pose, focusing on surrendering to God's love and letting go of any tension or stress.

Meditation:

Close your eyes and imagine God's love surrounding you like a warm, comforting blanket. As you breathe in, feel His love filling your heart. As you breathe out, let that love extend to others around you.

Scripture: Ecclesiastes 3:1
"There is a time for everything, and a season for every activity under heaven"

Reflection:
Patience is trusting that God's timing is perfect, even when we feel anxious or uncertain. Reflect on areas where you need to be more patient and how you can trust in God's timing.

Yoga Pose: Tree Pose (Vrksasana)
Pose Description:
• Stand tall, shift your weight onto your right foot, and bring the sole of your left foot to your inner right thigh or calf (avoid the knee).
• Bring your hands together at your heart or reach them overhead like branches.
• Focus on maintaining balance, just as you maintain faith in God's perfect timing.

Application:
• Reflect on a situation where you need to trust in God's timing.
• Consider how patience can help you grow spiritually.
• Practice Tree Pose, focusing on finding balance and patience in the pose.

Prayer:
"Lord, I trust in Your perfect timing. Teach me patience as I wait for Your plans to unfold. Help me to remain faithful and steadfast, knowing that You work all things for good. Amen."

Day 6: Seeking God's Guidance
Scripture: Psalm 32:8

"I will instruct you and teach you in the way you should go; I will
counsel you [who are willing to learn] with My eye upon you."

Reflection:

God's guidance is always available to us, but we must seek it actively.
Reflect on the areas of your life where you need His guidance and how
you can be more attuned to His voice.

Yoga Pose: Seated Forward Bend (Paschimottanasana)
Pose Description:

• Sit with your legs extended straight in front of you. Inhale as you
reach your arms up, lengthening your spine.
• Exhale as you fold forward from your hips, reaching for your feet or
shins.
• Focus on the stretch along your spine, and use this time to seek
God's guidance, listening for His still, small voice.

Application:
• Spend time in prayer, asking God for guidance in a specific
area.
• Reflect on how God has guided you in the past.
• Practice Seated Forward Bend, using the pose to focus on
humility and receptiveness to God's will.

Meditation:
In a quiet space, ask God for His guidance. Sit in silence for a
few moments, listening for His still, small voice. As you
breathe, imagine His light leading your path.

Day 7: Rest in God's Presence
Scripture: Matthew 11:28
"Come to me, all you who are weary and burdened, and I will
give you rest."

Reflection:
Rest is a vital part of our spiritual journey. Reflect on the
importance of rest and how you can find true rest in God's
presence, trusting Him to carry your burdens.

Yoga Pose: Corpse Pose (Savasana)
Pose Description:
• Lie flat on your back with your legs slightly apart and arms
resting by your sides, palms facing up.
• Close your eyes and focus on your breath, allowing your
body to completely relax.
• Use this time to rest in God's presence, releasing any stress,
worry, or tension, and feeling the peace that comes from
being fully surrendered to Him.

Application:
• Take a moment to rest in God's presence today, whether
through prayer, meditation, or simply sitting quietly.
• Reflect on areas of your life where you need to let go and
allow God to take control.
• Practice Corpse Pose, focusing on complete surrender and
trust in God's peace.

Prayer:
"Father, I come to You seeking rest for my soul. Help me to lay
down my burdens and find peace in Your presence. Remind me
that I am safe and secure in Your arms. Amen."

7. Faith in Motion

Day 8: Faith Over Fear
Scripture: Isaiah 41:10

"So do not fear, for I am with you; do not be dismayed, for I am your God. I will strengthen you and help you; I will uphold you with my righteous right hand."

Reflection:

Fear is natural, but it doesn't have to control us. God's presence and strength give us the courage to face our fears. Reflect on what fears you need to release today and how you can replace them with faith.

Yoga Pose: Eagle Pose (Garudasana)
Pose Description:
• Stand tall and bend your knees slightly.
• Wrap your right leg over your left and your right arm under your left, trying to touch your palms together.
• Focus on balance and stability as you hold the pose, embodying the strength to rise above fear with God's help.

Application:
• Identify a fear you want to release and ask God for the strength to overcome it.
• Reflect on past experiences where you've seen God's strength replace your fear.
• Practice Eagle Pose, focusing on balance and courage.

Meditation:
Focus on your breath, slowly inhaling and exhaling. As you breathe in, say to yourself, "I choose faith." As you breathe out, say, "I release fear." Let this rhythm calm your mind and strengthen your faith.

Day 9: God's Provision
Scripture: Matthew 6:26

"Look at the birds of the air; they do not sow or reap or store away in barns, and yet your heavenly Father feeds them. Are you not much more valuable than they?"

Reflection:

God provides for all our needs, just as He does for the birds and the flowers. Reflect on how God has provided for you in the past and trust Him for your future needs.

Yoga Pose: Half Moon Pose (Ardha Chandrasana)
Pose Description:

• Stand with your feet together, then step your right foot back into a lunge.
• Shift your weight onto your left foot and lift your right leg parallel to the floor, extending your left arm to the ground and right arm toward the sky.
• Focus on the balance and openness of the pose, symbolizing trust in God's provision.

Application:

• Write down ways God has provided for you in the past.
• Reflect on how you can trust Him for your current and future needs.
• Practice Half Moon Pose, focusing on balance and openness to receiving God's provision.

Prayer:

"Lord, thank You for being my provider. I trust that You will meet all my needs according to Your riches in glory. Help me to be content in every situation, knowing that You are my source. Amen."

Reflection:
Prayer is a powerful way to connect with God, and it should be a continuous part of our lives. Reflect on how you can make prayer a more integral part of your day.

Yoga Pose: Lotus Pose (Padmasana)
Pose Description:
• Sit cross-legged on the floor, bringing each foot to rest on the opposite thigh.
• Place your hands on your knees, palms facing up, in a gesture of openness.
• Focus on your breath and use this time to pray, inviting God's presence into your heart and mind.

Application:
• Incorporate more prayer into your daily routine.
• Reflect on the times in your life when prayer has made a difference.
• Practice Lotus Pose, using the time in the pose for focused, meditative prayer.

Meditation:
Spend a few minutes in silent prayer. Begin with gratitude, then move into intercession for others, and finally, listen quietly for God's response. Let your heart connect deeply with Him.

Day 11: God's Grace
Scripture: Ephesians 2:8-9
"For it is by grace you have been saved, through faith—and this is not from yourselves, it is the gift of God—not by works, so that no one can boast."

Reflection:
God's grace is a gift, not something we earn. Reflect on the areas of your life where you've experienced God's grace and how you can extend that grace to others.

Yoga Pose: Pigeon Pose (Eka Pada Rajakapotasana)
Pose Description:
• Start in Downward-Facing Dog, then bring your right knee forward and place it behind your right wrist.
• Extend your left leg straight back, keeping your hips square.
• Lower your upper body over your right leg, stretching your arms forward or resting them beside your body.
• Focus on the deep stretch and release, allowing yourself to fully receive and reflect on God's grace.

Application:
• Reflect on moments where you've seen God's grace in your life.
• Consider how you can show grace to others today.
• Practice Pigeon Pose, focusing on releasing tension and embracing the fullness of God's grace.

Prayer:
"Thank You, Lord, for Your amazing grace. I know I am unworthy, yet You love me and forgive me. Help me to live in that grace daily and to extend it to others. Amen."

Day 12: Living in Faith
Scripture: 2 Corinthians 5:7
"For we live by faith, not by sight."

Reflection:

Living by faith means trusting in what we cannot see and believing in God's promises. Reflect on how you can live more fully in faith today, trusting God's unseen hand in your life.

Yoga Pose: Bridge Pose (Setu Bandhasana)
Pose Description:

- Lie on your back with your knees bent and feet flat on the floor, hip-width apart.
- Press your feet into the floor and lift your hips toward the ceiling, keeping your arms by your sides.
- Focus on the stability and strength of the pose, embodying the act of living in faith, trusting in God's unseen support.

Application:

- Reflect on a situation where you need to trust God without seeing the full picture.
- Write down ways you can live more by faith and less by sight.
- Practice Bridge Pose, focusing on grounding yourself in faith.

Meditation:

Visualize yourself walking on a path guided by God's light. Each step is a step of faith, even when the way ahead is unclear. As you breathe, affirm, "I walk by faith, not by sight."

Day 13: God's Faithfulness
Scripture: Lamentations 3:22-23

"Because of the Lord's great love we are not consumed, for his compassions never fail. They are new every morning; great is your faithfulness."

Reflection:

God's faithfulness is unwavering, even when we falter. Reflect on how God has been faithful to you in the past and how you can trust in His faithfulness for your future.

Yoga Pose: Cobra Pose (Bhujangasana)
Pose Description:
- Lie face down with your hands placed under your shoulders.
- Inhale as you press into your hands, lifting your chest off the floor, keeping your elbows close to your body.
- Focus on the upward movement, symbolizing the renewal and faithfulness of God's love in your life.

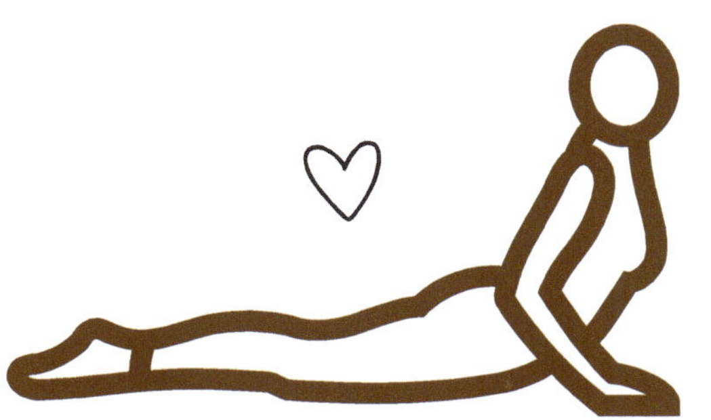

Application:
- Write down the ways God has shown His faithfulness to you.
- Reflect on how you can rely on His faithfulness in the future.
- Practice Cobra Pose, focusing on lifting your heart toward God and feeling the renewal of His faithfulness.

Prayer:
"Great is Your faithfulness, O Lord. You have been faithful in the past, and I trust You to be faithful in the future. Strengthen my faith as I remember Your steadfast love. Amen."

Day 14: Renewing Your Mind
Scripture: Romans 12:2

"Do not conform to the pattern of this world, but be transformed by the renewing of your mind. Then you will be able to test and approve what God's will is—his good, pleasing and perfect will."

Reflection:

Renewing your mind is an ongoing process of aligning your thoughts with God's truth. Reflect on the thoughts and beliefs you need to renew and how you can focus more on God's will in your life.

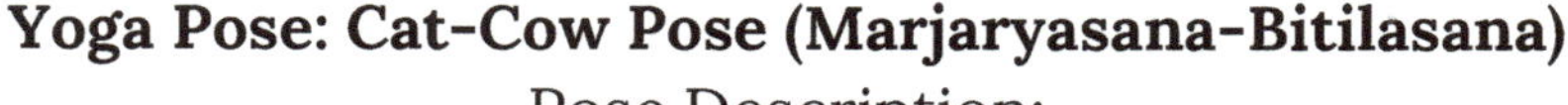

Yoga Pose: Cat-Cow Pose (Marjaryasana-Bitilasana)
Pose Description:
- Start on your hands and knees with your wrists under your shoulders and your knees under your hips.
- Inhale as you drop your belly toward the floor, lifting your gaze and tailbone (Cow Pose).
- Exhale as you round your spine toward the ceiling, tucking your chin to your chest (Cat Pose).
- Flow between these two poses, focusing on the rhythm of your breath and the renewal of your mind.

Application:
- Identify thoughts or beliefs that need to be renewed by God's truth.
- Reflect on how you can align your mind more closely with God's will.
- Practice Cat-Cow Pose, focusing on the renewal that comes with each breath and each movement.

Meditation:
As you breathe deeply, imagine God renewing your mind. Let go of old, negative thoughts and make space for new, positive ones based on His truth. Repeat, "I am being transformed by the renewal of my mind."

Day 15: God's Peace
Scripture: John 14:27

"Peace I leave with you; my peace I give you. I do not give to you as the world gives. Do not let your hearts be troubled and do not be afraid."

Reflection:

God's peace is a profound gift that surpasses all understanding. Reflect on how you can welcome this peace into your life, even amidst chaos and uncertainty.

Yoga Pose: Reclining Bound Angle Pose (Supta Baddha Konasana)

Pose Description:
• Lie on your back and bring the soles of your feet together, allowing your knees to fall open to the sides.
• Rest your arms by your sides, palms facing up, or place your hands on your belly.
• Focus on your breath, inviting God's peace to fill your mind and body as you relax into the pose.

Application:
• Reflect on situations where you need God's peace.
• Write down one way you can cultivate peace in your daily life.
• Practice Reclining Bound Angle Pose, allowing yourself to rest in the peace that God provides.

Prayer:

"Lord, I seek Your peace that surpasses all understanding. Calm my anxious heart and help me to rest in Your presence. May Your peace guard my heart and mind in Christ Jesus. Amen."

Day 16: Surrender to God
Scripture: Matthew 16:24

"Then Jesus said to his disciples, 'Whoever wants to be my disciple must deny themselves and take up their cross and follow me.'"

Reflection:

Surrendering to God means letting go of our own desires and trusting His plan. Reflect on what you need to surrender today to fully follow Christ.

Yoga Pose: Warrior I (Virabhadrasana I)

Pose Description:

• Stand with your feet wide apart. Turn your right foot out and your left foot slightly in, bending your right knee.

• Raise your arms overhead, palms facing each other, and gaze forward.

• Feel the strength and surrender in this pose, embodying the willingness to follow God's path.

Application:

• Identify an area of your life that you need to surrender to God.
• Reflect on what it means to take up your cross and follow Jesus.
• Practice Warrior I, focusing on the strength and surrender required to follow God's will.

Meditation:

As you sit quietly, visualize yourself placing your worries and desires into God's hands. Release them, trusting that He will take care of everything. Breathe deeply, feeling the peace that comes with surrender.

"If any of you lacks wisdom, you should ask God, who gives generously to all without finding fault, and it will be given to you."

Reflection:

God's wisdom is available to us if we seek it earnestly. Reflect on areas where you need God's wisdom and how you can be more open to His guidance.

Yoga Pose: Head-to-Knee Forward Bend (Janu Sirsasana)

Pose Description:
• Sit with your right leg extended and your left foot tucked against your inner right thigh.
• Inhale as you reach your arms overhead, and exhale as you fold forward, reaching for your right foot.
• Use this pose to focus on humility and the willingness to seek God's wisdom in all things.

Application:
• Ask God for wisdom in a specific situation.
• Reflect on how you can be more open to His guidance.
• Practice Head-to-Knee Forward Bend, using the pose as a time of reflection and seeking wisdom.

Prayer:
"Father, I need Your wisdom today. Guide my thoughts, decisions, and actions according to Your will. Help me to seek Your counsel in all I do. Amen."

Scripture: Colossians 3:12

"Therefore, as God's chosen people, holy and dearly loved, clothe yourselves with compassion, kindness, humility, gentleness and patience."

Reflection:

Compassion is a key element of living out our faith. Reflect on how you can show compassion to others, even in challenging situations.

Yoga Pose: Butterfly Pose (Baddha Konasana)

Pose Description:

• Sit with the soles of your feet together, allowing your knees to fall open to the sides.

• Hold your feet with your hands and sit up tall, focusing on lengthening your spine.

• Use this pose to cultivate a sense of openness and compassion, both toward yourself and others.

Application:

• Reflect on ways you can be more compassionate in your daily life.

• Consider someone who needs your kindness today and take action.

• Practice Butterfly Pose, focusing on opening your heart to others with compassion.

Meditation:

Focus on your heart as you breathe in compassion for yourself. As you exhale, imagine that compassion extending to others. Repeat the phrase, "May I be kind, may I be loving, may I be compassionate."

Scripture: Nehemiah 8:10
"Do not grieve, for the joy of the Lord is your strength."

Reflection:

God's joy is not dependent on our circumstances; it is a deep, abiding presence that strengthens us. Reflect on how you can tap into God's joy, even in difficult times.

Yoga Pose: Yogic Squat Pose (Malasana)
Pose Description:
• Start by standing with your feet a little wider than hip-width apart, toes slightly turned out.
• As you exhale, bend your knees and lower your hips down into a squat, bringing your torso between your thighs. Keep your heels grounded on the mat.
• Bring your palms together at your heart center in prayer position (Anjali Mudra), pressing your elbows gently against the inside of your knees to open your hips wider.
• Lengthen your spine, lifting your chest and crown of your head toward the ceiling while staying rooted in your feet.
• Focus on maintaining openness in your chest and grounding through your feet. Breathe deeply and fully, embracing the sense of stability and connection.

Application:
• Identify ways you can experience more joy in your daily life.
• Reflect on how God's joy has strengthened you in the past.
• Practice Yogic Squat Pose, letting go of stress and embracing the joy of the Lord.

Prayer:
"Thank You, Lord, for the joy that strengthens me. Help me to find joy in every circumstance, knowing that it is a gift from You. Let my joy be a witness to others of Your goodness. Amen."

Day 20: God's Forgiveness
Scripture: 1 John 1:9

"If we confess our sins, he is faithful and just and will forgive us our
sins and purify us from all unrighteousness."

Reflection:

God's forgiveness is a gift that purifies and renews us. Reflect on how
you can fully accept His forgiveness and extend that forgiveness to
others.

Yoga Pose: Reclining Twist (Supta Matsyendrasana)
Pose Description:

• Lie on your back, draw your right knee toward your chest, and
gently guide it across your body to the left side.
• Extend your right arm out to the side, turning your head to the
right.
• Focus on the release and purification that comes with this twist,
symbolizing God's forgiveness.

Application:

• Spend time in prayer, confessing any sins and accepting God's
forgiveness.
• Reflect on how you can extend forgiveness to someone in your
life.
• Practice Reclining Twist, focusing on the cleansing and
renewing power of God's forgiveness.

Meditation:

Imagine God's forgiveness washing over you like a gentle wave.
As you breathe in, feel His cleansing power. As you breathe out,
release any guilt or resentment you may be holding onto.

Day 21: Reflect and Rest
Scripture: Psalm 46:10
"He says, 'Be still, and know that I am God; I will be exalted among
the nations, I will be exalted in the earth.'"

Reflection:
Taking time to be still and reflect is essential for spiritual growth.
Reflect on how you can incorporate more moments of stillness
and reflection into your life.

Yoga Pose: Corpse Pose (Savasana)
Pose Description:
• Lie flat on your back with your legs slightly apart and arms
resting by your sides, palms facing up.
• Close your eyes and focus on your breath, allowing your body to
completely relax.
• Use this pose to rest in God's presence, reflecting on the lessons
of the past week and preparing your heart for what's to come.

Application:
• Spend extra time in reflection today, considering the themes
and lessons from the past week.
• Write down any insights or revelations that have come to you.
• Practice Corpse Pose, focusing on deep relaxation and spiritual
reflection.

Prayer:
"Lord, as I reflect on this week, I thank You for Your presence in
my life. Help me to rest in You, knowing that You are always with
me. Refresh my spirit and prepare me for the days ahead. Amen."

Day 22: God's Light
Scripture: Matthew 5:14-16

"You are the light of the world. A town built on a hill cannot be hidden. Neither do people light a lamp and put it under a bowl. Instead, they put it on its stand, and it gives light to everyone in the house. In the same way, let your light shine before others, that they may see your good deeds and glorify your Father in heaven."

Reflection:

We are called to be a light in the world, reflecting God's love and truth. Reflect on how you can let your light shine in your daily life.

Yoga Pose: Triangle Pose (Trikonasana)
Pose Description:
- Stand with your feet wide apart. Turn your right foot out and your left foot slightly in, aligning your heels.
- Extend your right arm forward and down, reaching for your shin or the floor, while your left arm reaches toward the sky.
- Focus on the expansiveness and openness of the pose, symbolizing the light you are called to shine.

Application:
- Reflect on how you can be a light in your community or workplace.
- Identify one way you can actively reflect God's love and truth today.
- Practice Triangle Pose, focusing on extending your light outward to others.

Meditation:
Visualize yourself as a vessel of God's light. As you breathe in, feel His light filling you. As you breathe out, imagine that light shining out into the world, touching those around you.

Day 23: Humility
Scripture: Philippians 2:3

"Do nothing out of selfish ambition or vain conceit. Rather, in humility value others above yourselves."

Reflection:

Humility is about putting others before ourselves and serving them with a heart of love. Reflect on how you can practice humility in your relationships and daily interactions.

Yoga Pose: Child's Pose (Balasana)
Pose Description:
- Kneel on the floor, touching your big toes together and sitting back on your heels.
- Lower your torso between your knees, extending your arms forward or resting them alongside your body.
- Focus on the humility and surrender of this pose, embodying the spirit of valuing others above yourself.

Application:
- Reflect on how you can practice humility in a specific relationship or situation.
- Consider an act of service you can do for someone today.
- Practice Child's Pose, focusing on the humility and surrender that comes with the pose.

Prayer:
"Lord, teach me to be humble like Christ. Help me to consider others before myself and to serve with a loving heart. Let my actions reflect Your humility. Amen."

Day 24: Perseverance
Scripture: James 1:12
"Blessed is the one who perseveres under trial because, having
stood the test, that person will receive the crown of life that the
Lord has promised to those who love him."

Reflection:
Perseverance is about standing firm in your faith, even in the
face of trials. Reflect on how you can strengthen your
perseverance in your spiritual journey.

Yoga Pose: Plank Pose (Phalakasana)
Pose Description:
• Start on your hands and knees, then step your feet back to
come into a straight line from head to heels.
• Engage your core, keeping your body strong and steady.
• Focus on the strength and endurance of this pose, symbolizing
the perseverance needed in your faith.

Application:
• Identify a trial or challenge where you need to persevere.
• Reflect on how you can strengthen your faith during
difficult times.
• Practice Plank Pose, focusing on building strength and
endurance.

Meditation:
As you breathe, focus on the word "persevere." Imagine
yourself climbing a mountain, taking one step at a time.
With each inhale, gather strength. With each exhale,
release any doubts.

Day 25: Gratitude
Scripture: 1 Thessalonians 5:18
"Give thanks in all circumstances; for this is God's will for you in Christ Jesus."

Reflection:

Gratitude is a powerful practice that shifts our focus from what we lack to what we have. Reflect on the blessings in your life and how you can cultivate an attitude of gratitude.

Yoga Pose: Heart Opening Pose (Anahatasana)
Pose Description:
• Begin on all fours in tabletop position with your hips directly over your knees and your shoulders over your wrists
• Slowly walk your hands forward, extending your arms out in front of you, while keeping your hips aligned above your knees
• Exhale, lower your chest, rest your forehead on the ground. Keep your elbows lifted, reaching forward with your fingertips.
• Focus on your breath, close your eyes. With each inhale, imagine your heart expanding with gratitude and with each exhale, release any negativity or tension.

Application:
• Start a gratitude journal, writing down three things you're thankful for each day.
• Reflect on how gratitude can transform your perspective.
• Practice Heart Opening Pose, using the pose to focus on surrender and thankfulness.

Prayer:
"Thank You, God, for the many blessings in my life. Help me to live with a grateful heart, appreciating all that You provide. May my gratitude overflow to bless others. Amen.

Day 26: Serving Others
Scripture: Mark 10:45
"For even the Son of Man did not come to be served, but to serve,
and to give his life as a ransom for many."

Reflection:
Serving others is at the heart of Jesus' teachings. Reflect on how
you can serve others in your daily life, following Christ's example of
selfless love.

Yoga Pose: Chair Pose (Utkatasana)
Pose Description:

• Stand with your feet together, then bend your knees as if sitting
back into a chair.
• Reach your arms overhead, keeping your chest lifted and spine
long. • Focus on the strength and stability of this pose, symbolizing
the readiness to serve others.

Application:
• Identify a specific way you can serve someone today.
• Reflect on how service to others is a reflection of
Christ's love.
• Practice Chair Pose, focusing on the strength and
commitment required to serve others.

Meditation:
Sit quietly and think of one person you can serve today.
Visualize yourself meeting their need with love and
kindness. As you breathe, let God's love flow through you,
preparing you to serve.

Day 27: Faith in God's Promises
Scripture: Hebrews 11:1

"Now faith is confidence in what we hope for and assurance about what we do not see."

Reflection:

Faith is trusting in God's promises, even when we don't see them fulfilled yet. Reflect on how you can strengthen your faith in God's promises and live with confident hope.

Yoga Pose: Half Lord of the Fishes Pose (Ardha Matsyendrasana)
Pose Description:
- Sit with your legs extended, then bend your right knee and cross your right foot over your left thigh.
- Inhale as you reach your left arm up, then exhale as you twist to the right, bringing your left elbow to the outside of your right knee.
- Focus on the twist, symbolizing the process of turning toward God's promises with faith.

Application:
- Reflect on a promise of God that you are waiting to see fulfilled.
- Consider how you can live with greater confidence and hope in His promises.
- Practice Half Lord of the Fishes Pose, using the twist to focus on turning toward God in faith.

Prayer:
"Lord, I stand on Your promises, knowing they are true. Help me to trust in what I cannot see, holding onto the hope that Your word will come to pass. Strengthen my faith today. Amen."

Day 28: Spiritual Renewal
Scripture: Isaiah 40:31
"But those who hope in the Lord will renew their strength. They will soar on wings like eagles; they will run and not grow weary, they will walk and not be faint."

Reflection:
Spiritual renewal comes from placing our hope in the Lord. Reflect on how you can experience renewal in your spiritual life and draw strength from God's presence.

Yoga Pose: Legs-Up-the-Wall Pose (Viparita Karani)
Pose Description:
• Sit sideways next to a wall, then swing your legs up the wall as you lie back, bringing your hips close to the wall.
• Rest your arms by your sides, palms facing up, and focus on your breath.
• Use this restorative pose to symbolize spiritual renewal and the renewal of your strength in God.

Application:
• Reflect on how you can experience spiritual renewal through prayer, worship, and time in God's presence.
• Identify an area of your life that needs renewal and ask God for strength.
• Practice Legs-Up-the-Wall Pose, focusing on rest, renewal, and the strength that comes from God.

Meditation:
Imagine yourself standing under a waterfall of God's love, feeling renewed and refreshed. As you breathe in, absorb His strength. As you breathe out, let go of anything that is holding you back from spiritual renewal.

Day 29: Joyful Living
Scripture: Psalm 118:24

"The Lord has done it this very day; let us rejoice today and be glad."

Reflection:

Living joyfully is a choice that reflects our gratitude and trust in God. Reflect on how you can live more joyfully each day, finding reasons to rejoice in God's goodness.

Yoga Pose: Reverse Warrior Pose (Viparita Virabhadrasana)
Pose Description:

• Begin in Warrior II, with your right foot forward and your left foot turned slightly out. Bend your right knee at a 90-degree angle, keeping your back leg strong and straight.
• Inhale as you lift your right arm up toward the ceiling, sweeping it back over your head. Allow your left hand to rest gently on the back of your left leg.
• Stretch through your right arm, creating a gentle arc with your upper body, while keeping your chest open and your torso lifted.
• Gaze up toward your lifted hand, or keep your gaze neutral if that feels more comfortable for your neck.
• Root down through both feet, maintaining stability in your legs as you reach back with your right arm and open through the side body.
• Breathe deeply, feeling the expansion and openness in your chest and heart, embodying a sense of joy and freedom.

Application:

• Reflect on ways you can bring more joy into your daily life.
• Write down moments of joy you've experienced and thank God for them.
• Practice Reverse Warrior Pose, focusing on balance, grace, and the joy of living in God's presence.

Prayer:

"Father, fill my heart with joy today. Let Your joy be my strength, and let it overflow to those around me. Help me to live each day with a joyful spirit, reflecting Your love. Amen."

Day 30: Commitment to Faith
Scripture: Joshua 24:15

"But if serving the Lord seems undesirable to you, then choose for yourselves this day whom you will serve, whether the gods your ancestors served beyond the Euphrates, or the gods of the Amorites, in whose land you are living. But as for me and my household, we will serve the Lord."

Reflection:
Commitment to faith is a daily choice to serve and follow God. Reflect on your commitment to living out your faith and how you can renew that commitment today.

Yoga Pose: Tree Pose (Vrksasana)
Pose Description:
- Stand tall, shift your weight onto your right foot, and bring the sole of your left foot to your inner right thigh or calf (avoid the knee).
- Bring your hands together at your heart or reach them overhead like branches.
- Focus on maintaining balance, just as you maintain your commitment to serve and follow God.

Application:
- Reflect on your commitment to faith and how you can renew it daily.
- Consider ways to involve your family or community in this commitment.
- Practice Tree Pose, focusing on grounding yourself in your commitment to serve the Lord.

Meditation:
As you sit quietly, recommit yourself to God. Visualize yourself standing firm in your faith, surrounded by God's love. Breathe deeply, feeling the strength of your commitment growing with each inhale.

Congratulations on completing "Faith in Motion: Connecting Spirit and Body." It's been a transformative journey, and I'm honored to have shared it with you. Over the past 30 days, we've explored the profound connection between our spiritual and physical selves, drawing closer to God through scripture and movement.

As you move forward, I encourage you to continue integrating these practices into your daily life. Reflect on the scriptures that spoke to you, the reflections that challenged you, and the yoga poses that brought you peace. Let these experiences remind you of the strength, love, and guidance that God provides.

Remember, this journey doesn't end here. Each day is an opportunity to deepen your faith, nurture your body, and live out the principles we've explored together. Keep seeking God's presence, trust in His timing, and let your faith guide your steps.

Thank you for joining me on this path. I pray that this devotional has enriched your spiritual and physical life, helping you to feel more connected, grounded, and inspired. May you continue to walk in faith, with a heart open to God's love and wisdom.

Blessings, Taprea

SCRIPTURE INDEX

Week 1: Foundation of Faith

Day 1: Trust in the Lord • Proverbs 3:5-6

Day 2: God's Strength • Philippians 4:13

Day 3: Faith and Action • James 2:17

Day 4: God's Love • 1 John 4:16

Day 5: Patience in God's Timing • Ecclesiastes 3:1

Day 6: Seeking God's Guidance • Psalm 32:8

Day 7: Rest in God's Presence • Matthew 11:28

Week 2: Strengthening Your Faith

Day 8: Faith Over Fear • Isaiah 41:10

Day 9: God's Provision • Matthew 6:26

Day 10: The Power of Prayer • 1 Thessalonians 5:17

Day 11: God's Grace • Ephesians 2:8-9

Day 12: Living in Faith • 2 Corinthians 5:7

Day 13: God's Faithfulness • Lamentations 3:22-23

Day 14: Renewing Your Mind • Romans 12:2

Week 3: Deepening Your Connection

Day 15: God's Peace • John 14:27

Day 16: Surrender to God • Matthew 16:24

Day 17: God's Wisdom • James 1:5

Day 18: Compassion • Colossians 3:12

Day 19: God's Joy • Nehemiah 8:10

Day 20: God's Forgiveness • 1 John 1:9

Day 21: Reflect and Rest • Psalm 46:10

Week 4: Living Out Your Faith

Day 22: God's Light • Matthew 5:14-16

Day 23: Humility • Philippians 2:3

Day 24: Perseverance • James 1:12

Day 25: Gratitude • 1 Thessalonians 5:18

Day 26: Serving Others • Mark 10:45

Day 27: Faith in God's Promises • Hebrews 11:1

Day 28: Spiritual Renewal • Isaiah 40:31

Day 29: Joyful Living • Psalm 118:24

Day 30: Commitment to Faith • Joshua 24:15

About the Author

Taprea is a devoted follower of Christ, a wife, mother, and yoga instructor passionate about helping others connect deeply with their faith through movement and mindfulness. With a background in health sciences and community health, she is set to complete her Master's degree in Business Administration in Spring 2025.

Taprea's journey into yoga began during one of the most challenging seasons of her life. Feeling lost and overwhelmed, she relied on her own understanding, leading to difficult circumstances. But even in those dark moments, she now sees how God was with her every step of the way. These challenges became an invitation to deepen her reliance on God's grace and guidance. Through prayer, she found a path to healing, service, and growth.

Her time at Reflections Yoga Studio was transformative. Each humble task—whether cleaning mats or sweeping floors—became an act of worship, a way to honor God and prepare a sacred space for others. These physical acts mirrored her inner journey, where she cleared away fear and doubt to make room for God's peace.

This experience has shaped Taprea's understanding of faith and movement as intertwined elements of her spiritual life. Through daily yoga practice, woven with scripture and prayer, she has found a tangible, embodied way to live out her faith. It is this deep, personal experience that she brings to "Faith in Motion," inviting others to discover the powerful connection between spirit and body.

With this devotional, Taprea offers a path to healing, strength, and a deeper connection with God—one breath, one movement, and one prayer at a time.